Life Cycles

Life Cycle of a Frog

by Meg Gaertner

www.focusreaders.com

Copyright © 2022 by Focus Readers®, Lake Elmo, MN 55042. All rights reserved. No part of this book may be reproduced or utilized in any form or by any means without written permission from the publisher.

Focus Readers is distributed by North Star Editions:
sales@northstareditions.com | 888-417-0195

Produced for Focus Readers by Red Line Editorial.

Photographs ©: Shutterstock Images, cover, 1, 21; iStockphoto, 4, 7, 8, 11, 13, 14, 17, 18

Library of Congress Cataloging-in-Publication Data
Names: Gaertner, Meg, author.
Title: Life cycle of a frog / by Meg Gaertner.
Description: Lake Elmo, MN : Focus Readers, [2022] | Series: Life
  cycles | Includes index. | Audience: Grades 2-3
Identifiers: LCCN 2021003756 (print) | LCCN 2021003757 (ebook) | ISBN
  9781644938287 (hardcover) | ISBN 9781644938744 (paperback) | ISBN
  9781644939208 (ebook) | ISBN 9781644939642 (pdf)
Subjects: LCSH: Frogs--Life cycles--Juvenile literature.
Classification: LCC QL668.E2 G339 2022 (print) | LCC QL668.E2 (ebook) |
  DDC 597.8/9156--dc23
LC record available at https://lccn.loc.gov/2021003756
LC ebook record available at https://lccn.loc.gov/2021003757

Printed in the United States of America
Mankato, MN
082021

About the Author

Meg Gaertner enjoys reading, writing, dancing, and being outside. She lives in Minnesota.

Table of Contents

CHAPTER 1
Egg 5

CHAPTER 2
Tadpole 9

THAT'S AMAZING!
Big Changes 12

CHAPTER 3
Metamorphosis 15

CHAPTER 4
Frog 19

Focus on Frog Life Cycles • 22
Glossary • 23
To Learn More • 24
Index • 24

Chapter 1

Egg

Frogs start as eggs. Eggs form when two adult frogs **mate**. Then the **female** frog lays the eggs. She lays them in a pond or in other fresh water.

The eggs are tiny. They might float in the water. They might stick to plants. Or they might fall to the bottom of the pond.

Fun Fact

The **male** frog often helps care for the eggs. For example, he might carry the eggs to safety.

Chapter 2

Tadpole

The eggs **hatch**. Tadpoles come out. A tadpole is a frog **larva**. It has a short, round body. It has a flat tail.

Tadpoles have gills. Gills are tiny openings in the skin. Tadpoles breathe underwater with their gills. Tadpoles also have small mouths. They eat plants in the water.

Fun Fact A tadpole is also called a polliwog.

That's Amazing!

Big Changes

Tadpoles are very different from frogs. Tadpoles live only underwater. They have tails and gills. They eat plants. Frogs spend most of their time on land. They have no tails or gills. And they eat animals such as insects. Big changes turn a tadpole into a frog. These changes are called a **metamorphosis**.

Chapter 3

Metamorphosis

The tadpole changes over time. These changes might take two weeks. They might take up to three years. It depends on the type of frog.

A tadpole's gills and tail disappear. Front and back legs grow instead. **Lungs** grow inside the tadpole. They will help it breathe air. When the metamorphosis ends, a young frog steps onto land.

Fun Fact

Frogs are amphibians. That means they can live both on land and in water.

Chapter 4

Frog

Frogs have strong back legs for jumping. They have **webbed** feet for swimming. Their eyes stick out from their heads. They have flat ears.

Frogs need to stay wet. So, most frogs live near fresh water. Some frogs dig into the ground. Other frogs live in trees.

About once a year, frogs mate. The females lay eggs. The life cycle begins again.

Fun Fact

Frogs do not drink water like humans do. Instead, they take in water through their skin.

Life Cycle Stages

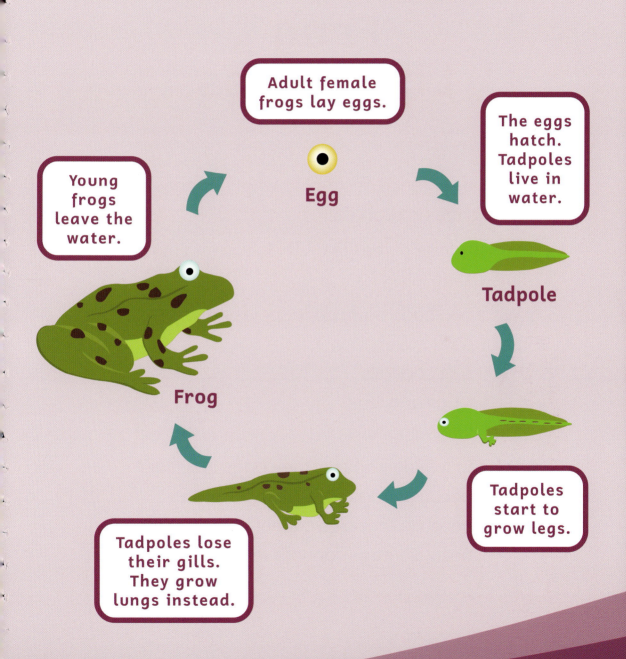

FOCUS ON

Frog
Life Cycles

Write your answers on a separate piece of paper.

1. Write a sentence describing what happens during metamorphosis.

2. Which stage of the life cycle do you find most interesting? Why?

3. What two body parts do tadpoles have that frogs don't have?
   - A. gills and tails
   - B. lungs and legs
   - C. lungs and tails

4. Why do female frogs lay their eggs in water?
   - A. because frogs only live in the water
   - B. because tadpoles cannot live on land
   - C. because frogs cannot live on land

Answer key on page 24.

Glossary

female
Able to have babies or lay eggs.

hatch
To break open so a young animal can come out.

larva
The young form of an animal that goes through a metamorphosis.

lungs
Body parts that some animals use to breathe air.

male
Unable to have babies or lay eggs.

mate
To come together to make a baby.

metamorphosis
A change from a young form to a completely different adult form.

webbed
Having toes that are connected by skin.

To Learn More

BOOKS

Dunn, Mary R. *A Frog's Life Cycle*. North Mankato, MN: Capstone Press, 2018.

London, Martha. *Bullfrogs*. Lake Elmo, MN: Focus Readers, 2021.

NOTE TO EDUCATORS

Visit **www.focusreaders.com** to find lesson plans, activities, links, and other resources related to this title.

Index

E
eggs, 5–6, 9, 20–21

F
female, 5, 20–21

G
gills, 10, 12, 16, 21

L
lungs, 16, 21

M
metamorphosis, 12, 16

T
tadpoles, 9–10, 12, 15–16, 21

Answer Key: 1. Answers will vary; **2.** Answers will vary; **3.** A; **4.** B